Mosaic of the Soul

By

M. L. Rocco

Mosaic of the Soul

Cover design and interior artwork by M. L. Rocco.

First Edition, 2025.

ISBN 979-8-218-65691-1

For the boy with red hair and a quiet heart –

I wandered for years without a home,

until you opened your arms and made one.

Now, even in silence or stillness,

I carry the calm of you with me.

"I can be changed by what happens to me. But I refuse to be reduced by it."

– Maya Angelou

Table of Contents

Prologue

Part I: Shattered Foundations

Part II: Cracks in the Mirror

Part III: A Silent Void

Part IV: Fragments of Resilience

Part V: Rewoven Threads

Epilogue

Prologue

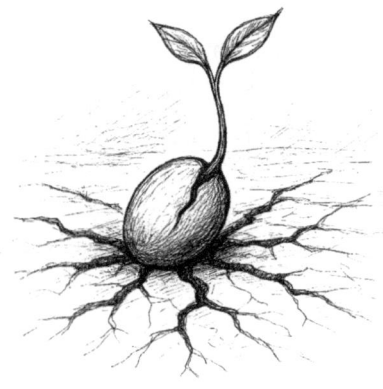

Before the words begin, before the ink stains the page, there was a child, shattered and whole all at once. A story woven from pieces that don't always fit, held together by the smallest strands of hope. This is not just a journey through pain but through survival – an exploration of what it means to piece ourselves back together, even when we feel shattered beyond repair. In these pages, you'll find fragments of my story, raw and tender, broken and rebuilt. And somewhere between the lines, perhaps, you'll find echoes of your own.

To the One Who Survived

To the one who was born among fractures,

who learned to speak in echoes and silence –

I see you.

You have worn shadows like a second skin,

carried the weight of hands that should have held you gently,

built a home inside the wreckage of love.

You have lost and lost and lost,

and yet –here you are.

This is not the story of what was taken,

but of what remains.

Not just the breaking, but the binding,

the hands that gather shattered things,

piecing them into something whole.

Step forward.

The mosaic is waiting.

Part I: Shattered Foundations

Somewhere between the laughter of childhood and the ache of experience, the first cracks begin to form. The foundations we stand upon are often built from pain – a mosaic of fragmented moments, half-remembered but ever-present, shaping each step we take. There are things in the dark that no child should know, secrets that cling like shadows, becoming as natural as breath. It was here I first learned the meaning of survival – though survival often meant becoming something I was never meant to be. The pieces of my past remain jagged, sharp, and unrelenting. Yet somehow, despite it all, they still form the shape of me.

Behind the Locked Door

In a world aglow with childhood's play,

a little girl, just seven, would often stray.

Into rooms where laughter turned hollow, too thin,

where secrets whispered soft and shadows crept in.

"Special playtime," he called it, wrapped in deceit,

a bond unmade by blood, but trust incomplete.

With her stepbrother commanding, innocence swayed,

behind locked doors, a sinister game was played.

She slipped through the veil, naivety her guide,

unaware of the darkness, of the danger inside.

There, in that silence, her spirit shrank small,

as her brother held power, she felt none at all.

One fateful day, with a grin, came the call,

he invited her brother, drawn into the thrall.

But the boy felt a chill that devoured the light,

With courage unbidden, he rushed to the fight.

He told of the secrets wrapped tight in their hearts,

hoping the truth might unravel the parts.

But the parents denied it, with shame in their name,

all three children punished; their innocence framed.

"Never speak of this," like dirt swept beneath rugs,

they swept it away with their whispers and shrugs.

Years folded like pages, yet silence remained,

a house full of shadows, connection estranged.

As time passed, her mind began to see,

the weight of what should have never been.

The threads of childhood, now tangled and torn,

each memory layered with guilt, with scorn.

Now in her solitude, she learned to conceal,

finding comfort alone, where the wounds could heal.

Yet still, with each heartbeat, the ghosts linger near,

innocence slipping, forever unclear.

She weaves a new tale from the threads of pain,

finding strength in shadows, where light once had waned.

For every child's laughter holds stories untold,

and through the darkness, resilience unfolds.

Echoes of Silence

Somewhere between the laughter and the ache,

the first cracks formed, too deep to shake.

A house built on silence, cracked and cold,

where warmth was rare, and love turned old.

I learned to survive, not by love but by fear,

shrinking smaller each time someone drew near.

The bruises, like secrets, I learned to hide,

a silent scream that echoed inside.

My father's love was a fist, not a hand,

a battle fought, but I couldn't understand.

I was the shadow, always in the way,

yearning for love that would never stay.

And she, my mother, drowning in her pain,

poured her sorrow, again and again.

Her broken heart became my only song,

a weight too heavy for someone so young.

I held her tears, but couldn't keep mine,

I became the keeper of scars, not divine.

Her battles were hers, but I felt each blow,

caught in the storm, with nowhere to go.

I grew older, but never got free,

trapped in a mirror I couldn't see.

Survival became my only fight,

a puzzle of pieces not ever right.

Still, somehow, I stand, jagged but whole,

a mosaic of pieces that make up my soul.

My scars sing louder than silence allows,

a testament carved into all I am now.

Mosaic of Struggles

In shadows deep, where silence clings,

a child's laughter lost to broken strings.

Beneath the weight of storms concealed,

a heart encased; my spirit sealed.

Under hands that once brought pain,

I learned to rise, though broken again.

A bearer of burdens, courage worn thin,

nestled in sorrow, where shadows begin.

Whispers of darkness sway through the night,

ticking clocks echo a lingering fright.

With each tick, a memory's weight,

shadows that creep where hope deflates.

In the quiet of those early years,

I learned to carry burdens, mute my fears.

Yet still, I stood, though bruised and torn,

a child, fractured, though battle-worn.

Fists have fallen, words have left marks,

and I am a mosaic of fractured sparks.

Through loops of anguish, chains tightly worn,

a spirit once vibrant, now battered and torn.

With every misstep, with every lament,

I rise from the gloom, though days are spent.

Though anxiety whispers and dread linger close,

I summon the remnants of courage, a ghost.

Each scar tells a story, each tear a release,

in the field of my battles, I ache for peace.

Sober I stand, with grief in my veins,

a warrior's heart where the weariness reigns.

To the struggles that shaped my disguise,

to the storms I endured, to the silence that lies.

In the tapestry woven, my battles unfold,

I shimmer like dusk – but the warmth feels cold.

Part II: Cracks in the Mirror

Love should be soft, yet it often leaves jagged edges. The reflection in the mirror is rarely what we wish to see; it's sometimes shattered, cracked, and distorted by hands that never bothered to heal it. In these pieces, I explore the ways we come to believe we are not enough – how others rewrite the story of our worth, and we let them. Love is a struggle; the pull between what we give and what we receive. In this battle, we often lose ourselves. These moments, like ghosts, haunt us – echoes of tenderness that leave more scars than they soothe.

Stuck in the Cycle

I was your first, your softest lie,

the one you'd leave, then circle back by.

You took my love, and gave it none,

yet I returned, for I was undone.

Your hands, they wandered – always away,

to other girls who made you stay.

They were nothing, just reflections,

while I became your deepest connection.

I held your pain, your broken nights,

memorized your schedule, made things right.

I saw the best you tried to hide,

but you always chose the ones who lied.

You called me when you couldn't breathe,

crying through the grief you'd never leave.

Your mother's ghost still pulled you near,

but I, your anchor, disappeared.

I was the shadow in your wake,

while you loved her, for her sake.

The girl who never saw the cracks,

while I kept you, always looking back.

You called me "a mistake" in the light of day,

but I endured because you pleaded, I stay.

You hurt me more with every touch,

yet I gave you everything, asking for so much.

And still, I let you come and go,

a side piece in the life you chose to sow.

I helped you rise, helped you fall,

yet, you didn't care to give me anything at all.

You used to me to heal your broken parts,

while tearing mine apart with darts.

You gave her your love, your strength, your name,

but I was the one left to bear the shame.

Reflections in Fracture

On the cusp of dusk, a dance of dreams,

prom night shimmered, fractured seams.

A crown of despair weighed softly tight,

in a room filled with echoes, I battled the night.

Laughter turned hollow, reflections of pain,

friendships like shadows, dancing in rain.

A battle of secrets, my heart in a vise,

as I searched through the fragments, I did not think twice.

Triple C's whispered, the vodka sang low,

with my mom's heart pills, I surrendered to woe.

Thoughts spiraled, whispers too soft to be heard,

then screamed in the silence, every voice blurred.

In love's jagged grip, I thought I was free –

but the mirror distorted the truth meant for me.

Falling like autumn leaves, I crumbed, I wept,

while the façade of perfection sank deeper, I crept.

The pills slipped through my fingers, their promise a lie,

each swallow a silence, a soft lullaby.

Yet a hand held on tight, cutting through haze,

rushing cold water, igniting the blaze.

Though silence surrounded, I felt tender care,

a bond forged in shadows – a truth we would share.

But today I stand, a ghost of what's real,

haunted by echoes of pain I concealed.

Each jagged reflection, each moment of strife,

a reminder of battles, shadows of life.

So, I linger in struggle, embrace what I've braved,

in the cracks of the mirror, my spirit's enslaved.

Though fear may still linger, I cannot retreat,

I've danced with the dark and stayed on my feet.

Life's tender whispers still call me along,

I hear them now - soft, but fierce, and strong.

The Eyes that Follow

In the twilight of youth, love wore a fragile mask,

a shimmering façade, too dazzling to unmask.

You entered like wildfire, igniting a spark,

but shadows loomed heavy, leaving scars in the dark.

Clingy hands tore at the fabric of dreams,

every whisper of doubt, unraveling seams.

Fights morphed to fury; your rage grew so tall,

in the mirrors of chaos, I felt myself fall.

In the heat of the moment, I froze in my place,

fear wrapped around me, a cold, tight embrace.

Your eyes held the tempest, reflecting my dread,

a fractured mosaic where love once had led.

When distance turned bitter and haunting became,

you lingered like echoes that called out my name.

Outside my job's door, your presence was fraught,

each heartbeat a reminder of battles fought.

Days bled into nights – lost in the chase,

caught in the struggle of love's cruel embrace.

Then news drifted softly, like whispers of fate,

you lost your own battle; I felt no weight.

Your struggles fell silent, now shadows long gone,

a chapter closed gently, a fading dawn.

Though memories tangled in shadows would creep,

I chose to let go, as the past fell asleep.

No longer a victim of love's jagged song,

I reclaim the echoes where I still belong.

From the remnants of anguish, unresolved and raw,

I trace the reflections of what I once saw.

For love can be lessons, unkind and unclear,

mirrors may distort and reveal all my fears.

Yet in these cracked verses, where truths intertwine,

I linger in silence, in the echoes of time.

Voices in the Shadows

In shadows deep where silence grew,

a gaze once tender, now a cage I knew.

Chains unseen, a heart ensnared,

whispered threats, my soul laid bare.

Boundaries drawn, a fragile plea,

but love turned dark, no longer free.

With every fight, a piece would break,

my self was lost, for your love's sake.

Among the friends, masks would wear,

a fragile laugh, suffused with care.

"Change for me," the whispers said,

while fear crept in, and hope lay dead.

The walls echoed with screams of pain,

a heart unbound, yet bound in chains.

Screams and bottles, panic's call,

in a cluttered home where shadows fall.

A fading frame, skin stretched thin,

in every bruise, a bottle's din.

"Better you stay," the words they said,

escape, he swore, and I'd be dead.

But strength emerged from shattered glass,

with trembling hands, I made the pass.

A phone call made, a silent vow,

to pack my dreams, reclaim the now.

I stood alone, a fractured shell,

a hollow echo I knew too well.

The path to healing, jagged and slow,

where every step feels like sinking low.

And still, the echoes never cease,

the remnants of the chains won't release.

No phoenix rises from this pain –

the weight, the wounds, they still remain.

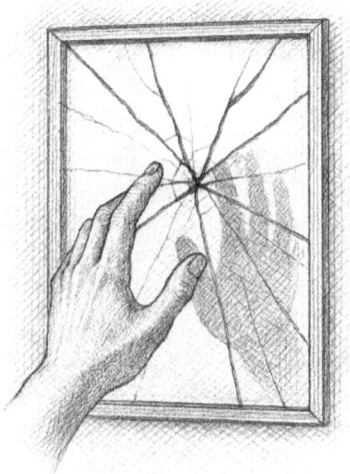

Tangled in the Mirror

I gave you pieces, soft and true,

hoping you'd shape them into you.

But your love was jagged, cold and sharp,

a constant storm that left its mark.

I wore your silence, carried your weight,

managing dreams while I lost my state.

Your family's love, a mirror too bright,

made me feel broken, fading from sight.

I was your mother, your guiding hand,

while you took, I tried to understand.

I gave you time, I gave you care,

but in the end, you were never there.

I held your hopes, your music's soul,

but you took my strength, left me a hole.

When my body broke, you stepped away,

told me my pain was just in the way.

You promised me love, you promised a life,

a house, a child, a future as a wife.

But each time I asked, you turned away,

with empty promises that led me astray.

I stood beside you, watching you rise,

while I sank deeper, masked by your lies.

You chose your type, left me in doubt,

made me feel like I wasn't enough, wore me out.

I gave you love; I gave you space,

yet you let me fall from my own place.

When I asked for a pause, I asked for rest,

you moved on quickly, put me to the test.

But now I see through the cracks in the glass,

you never loved me, not as I asked.

Your songs speak lies, of pain you claim,

while I was your muse, you erased my name.

I'll no longer bend, no longer break,

I'm gathering pieces for my own sake.

The mirror may crack, but I'll build it right,

I am enough, even without the fight.

Part III: A Silent Void

Grief does not arise with a cry, but with a silence so deafening it drowns out the loudest voices. There are losses that cannot be named – not because they are unseen, but because they are too vast to be contained by mere words. In the emptiness they leave behind, I have sought meaning, but it remains elusive, a void that refuses to be filled. Pieces of my heart are buried in spaces I can never reach, yet the weight of that absence lingers, lingering in the stillness between breaths. It pulses in those quiet moments when the world moves on, but I remain frozen, cradling the grief of what never came to pass.

Unseen Bonds

In a tender dream of life anew,

two tiny souls, I cherish you.

Tough stars align and plans are laid,

your presence lingers, a love unswayed.

On March the third, the world turns gray,

a path I thought was clear, now swept away.

Twins in my heart, what could have been,

a journey begun, yet never seen.

We weren't prepared, the choice made clear,

but in your absence, I feel you near.

As time unfolds, my heart begins to yearn,

could my resolve have shifted, a different turn?

Two beautiful boys, like whispers in dreams,

with laughter and giggles, and radiant beams.

At a baby shower, a moment so rare,

a mother spoke softly, as if she could share:

"I see two boys, watching over you,"

a message of hope, in skies so blue.

Elio and Luca, my guiding light,

in shadows of sorrow, you shine so bright.

September's promise, now wrapped in dreams,

of cradled laughter and soft baby schemes.

Though I may not hold you, you'll never depart,

for you live forever, within my heart.

Through grief and healing, I carry your name,

in love's gentle whisper, I'm never the same.

Dear Elio and Luca, confusion entwined,

in your quiet absence, my heart's redefined.

A Name in the Wind

In a new space, shadows flicker and dance,

where laughter once bloomed, now haunted by chance.

From the ashes of longing, a flicker ignites,

a fleeting connection that softens the nights.

But beneath the bright surface, a tempest unfurls,

life's cruel twist weaving through heartbeats and swirls.

An endless cycle, a gift intertwined,

yet hope bears a weight, heavy on the mind.

January dawns, with a chill in the air,

an unbidden journey, a call to despair.

In sterile halls where silence clings tight,

a flicker of life fades into the night.

Aranea, sweet child, a dream never born,

your name on my lips, in my heart, a soft thorn.

I picture your smile, a mirror of me,

a little girl dancing in fields wild and free.

But fate, cold and distant, in shadows would creep,

a lesson in loss, a heartache so deep.

In whispers of sorrow, no one to confide,

I carry this burden, alone, I survive.

Ectopic echoes of what could have been,

a chance for tomorrow, not traced in the skin.

Yet here in my heart, you reside as pure light,

a name like a lullaby, soothing the night.

So, here's to the moments that flickered and fell,

in the story of us, a tale hard to tell.

Though you never took breath in this world of our pain,

Aranea, sweet spirit, I'll honor your name.

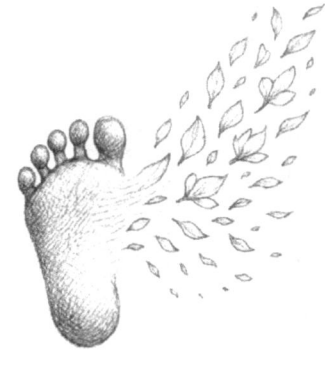

Between Light and Shadow

In March's soft whispers, a promise turned cold,

two lives intertwined, but their story untold.

Elio, cherished, Luca, my light,

forever your memory guiding me through the night.

With every heartbeat, your absence still stings,

in the echoes of silence, my longing takes wing.

Then January's chill, in the shadows it stole,

Aranea, dear daughter, who still fills my soul.

A path carved by fate, heavy with loss,

in the pattern of time, your love is the cost.

I stand on the edge of a desolate shore,

where shadows whisper, and memories roar.

A yearning for solace, a desperate plea,

to drown in the haze or set my spirit free.

Yet here in the darkness, despair holds its reign,

the love for those lost haunts me like chains.

Though they drift in the silence, so far from my call,

in dreams, I still seek them, in the depths of my fall.

So, I breathe in my sorrow; let it claim me whole,

each tear that I carry, a weight on my soul.

In the stillness of night, in the cold of the sun,

Elio, Luca, Aranea – my three little ones.

In anguish, I gather the love we once shared,

their spirits entwined with the burdens I bared.

For though I may stumble through shadows I roam,

in sorrow, I linger, far from my home.

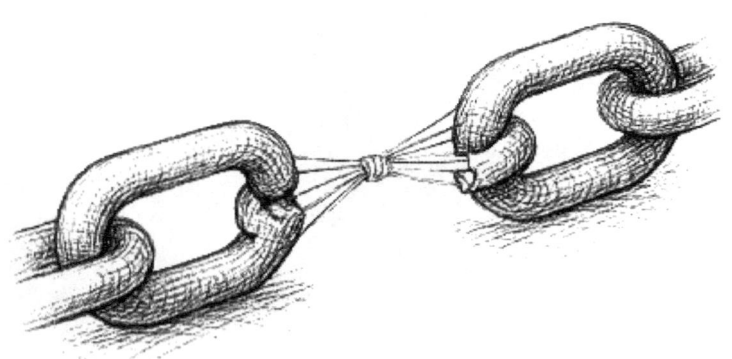

Part IV: Fragments of Resilience

In the ashes of what was, a spark flickers. We are not born of perfection, but shaped by the fragments left behind after the storm. Resilience is not a seamless whole – it's the slow, painful process of stitching together what's been shattered. It's found in the brokenness, the failures, the grief we carry. Yet, there is beauty in the rebuilding, even when every step feels heavy and the scares tug.

And still, as I rise from the rubble, I feel the weight of what came before. The journey is never a straight line – healing is jagged, erratic, full of setbacks. Strength isn't drawn from some untouchable well; it's built, piece by piece, through every trial and fall. Somewhere along the way, I learned that even in the cracks, there's room to stand again, to breathe, to reclaim what's left. Even with a broken foundation, I find my feet and step forward, knowing the path may be fractured – but it is mine to walk.

Fragments of Hope

In shadows thick, my heart does ache,

with silent cries, the night forsakes.

A childhood fractured, a realm of pain,

in the depths of dark, I learned to feign.

A stepbrother's touch, a brother's disdain,

with fists of fear, my spirit's pain.

A father's fury, a tempest's cry,

in brutal moments, I learned to hide.

With burdens crushing, I wore my guise,

a plea unheard, beneath distant skies.

Through storms of sorrow, on endless seas,

I faced the trials, but found no ease.

An alcoholic's chains, a mother's woe,

in muted silence, my fears would grow.

From toxic ties that twisted my mind,

a threat to lock me away, confined.

Dreams of life lost, twins swept away,

then came the ectopic darkness to play.

Yet through the sorrow, I walked, but lost,

a survivor's soul, but at what cost?

With every fall, I bent with pain,

each scar reminder of love's disdain.

Through anxiety's choke and torment's jest,

I've learned of struggle, but not of rest.

A landscape marred with shadows long,

I cling to my truth, though the end feels wrong.

So here I linger, strength worn thin,

a tale of endurance, masked from within.

From ashes I crawl, burdened by fear,

searching for warmth in the frost of the year.

Through trembling nights and hollowed skies,

I gather the pieces that refuse to die.

Whispers of the Past

Two years, one month, twenty-two days,

a journey through the smoke, lost in the haze.

Once I danced beneath brighter lights,

now shadows creep and haunt my nights.

In quiet hours, as dusk descends,

the echoes of past choices are like old friends.

A bottle's call, a cigarette's embrace,

in dreams, they linger, a shadow I can't face.

With each new dawn, the urge returns,

an ember glowing, a gut that churns.

What solace found in fleeting release,

when every taste brings me to my knees?

I recall the chains, the weight they bore,

yet here I stand, still wanting more.

Though scars remain from battles fought,

I chase the peace I never caught.

So, I navigate these long, dark nights,

with hope flickering beneath dim lights.

For every dream that tempts my plight,

a war within, I must face each night.

With every step, shadows loom,

a testament to battles lost, not won too soon.

For the path I tread is steep and wide,

but an aching heart still stands beside.

Navigating the Storm

In the mirror, a shadow whispers life,

reflections of battles etched in thin skin.

Haunted by echoes of past pain and strife,

each glance a reminder of where I have been.

The world outside, a labyrinth of dread,

footsteps echo, the pulse of the street.

A fear I can't shake, the terror of tread,

wondering if strangers will turn into creeps.

Will I face the gaze of my toxic past?

A predator lurking in the light of day?

Or feel the chains of those memories cast,

binding my heart, keeping courage at bay.

Each trip to the door, a mountain to climb,

will I seize the moment or hide in the night?

The thoughts circle round in a rhythm, a rhyme,

as the weight of my burdens obscures my sight.

My heart beats loudly beneath layers of clothes,
constricted by echoes of "less is more" lore.
Heels that once signaled a confident pose,
now jagged reminders of what I abhor.

Seizures lie dormant, lurking in black,
an unseen thief in my safety's embrace.
With each step I ponder, will I turn back?
To a life embroiled in fear, in disgrace.

Yet amidst the chaos, resilience flickers,
a spark in the darkness longing to bloom.
I'm more than the fragments, more than the snickers,
I'll rise from the ashes; I'll fill up the room.

Though mirrors may tremble with scars from the past,
I reclaim my reflection, piece by piece.
With each deep breath, I shatter the cast,
and I'll learn to step forward, to finally find peace.

A Heart Unfurled

In the stillness of my hidden storm,

through silence worn like a second skin.

I let my scars breathe, their stories warm,

hoping for a glance, a sign from within.

"I need therapy," I said, feeling rain,

but dad asked me, "What troubles your mind?

You have all you could want – how can this pain?"

In his world of plenty, my heart felt confined.

Mom's worried gaze, a lighthouse in my night,

with whispers soft, "What's weighing your soul?"

But father's icy words cut deep within their bite,

"You're not my daughter," a fracture to console.

Mad I kept silent, my struggles held tight,

while shadows grew longer, my heart felt with strain.

But strength bloomed in therapy, a flickering light,

I drew a firm line and reclaimed my own name.

Then came a moment, a twist in the tale,
secrets unraveling from the therapist's lips.
The bond that I cherished began to derail,
their link to my story, like ice, it would slip.

So, I stopped the sessions, retreated from sight,
from vulnerability that dared me to grow.
Gathering pieces, my pain put to flight,
navigating shadows, unlearning the flow.

Yet through the fractures, resilience ignites,
to redefine family, to reclaim my fight.
Though trust may still tremor, and emotions take flight,
I'm learning to stand in the stillness of night.

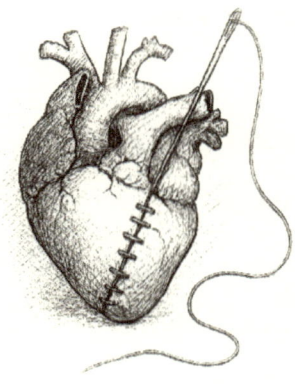

Tapestry of Resilience

In life's intricate tapestry, threads fray and break,

with every unraveling, my spirit finds its way.

Stitches of struggle, a truth I can't fake,

crafting a canvas from battles each day.

From shadows of doubt, whispers rise in the dark,

anxiety dances like flickers at the edge of my sight.

Silent burdens linger, a constant, subtle mark,

yet within this weave, I strive to find light.

The weight of my body betrays me at times,

storms within twist like daggers in my chest.

Seemingly endless, the shifts and the climbs,

yet even in turmoil, I strive to be my best.

A body that bends where it shouldn't begin,

the storms continue, my body, a ship.

Each movement an ache that burns from within,

struggling through winds that cause me to slip.

Endless battles leave their scars behind,

yet through the wear, I gather what's mine.

A face in the mirror that time can't rewind,

transforming the pain into strength by design.

The earth spins beneath my feet, my pulse racing with the shift,

a thief in the night steals pieces of my control.

But even in the chaos, I continue to drift,

learning the rhythm, making myself whole.

A hollow hunger, as though the world has taken more than it gave,

I gather the shards of me, piece by fragile piece.

Through the wear and tear, through every wave,

I reclaim my essence, my soul's quiet peace.

So here stands my heart, weary and raw,

every struggle is a testament in the book of my soul.

In this woven tapestry, I embrace each flaw,

resilience burns bright; through it, I am whole.

Part V: Rewoven Threads

Healing is rarely loud or triumphant. It is often a quiet act, unseen and uncertain, like stitching together threads that once seemed too frayed to hold. Here, I am learning that healing is not about forgetting what broke me, but about living alongside it – carrying the weight without letting it consume me.

Some days, I still stumble. Some days, my garden wilts despite my best efforts. But I am learning that it's not failure – it's simply the nature of growth. The threads I hold are not perfect, and neither am I, but they are mine. And that, I think, is enough.

So, I plant. I nurture. I stumble and begin again. I trust that even in the darkest soil, something can bloom. And though healing is not linear, I am learning to breathe in the uncertainty – knowing that one day, this garden will flourish, simply because I did not give up.

The Garden Begins Again

I have pulled the weeds of days long dead,

Tangled in sorrow and words unsaid.

My hands are calloused, but certain and sure,

and I sow new seeds, patient and pure.

The soil still aches from things I've lost,

but I plant anyway, despite the cost.

Some days the blooms fall under despair,

some days I'll forget how to tend with care.

The garden is mine, and mine alone,

but I am still learning how seeds are sown.

Not all will flourish, and some will decay,

but I'll keep planting anyway.

The growth is not perfect, the colors are few,

but life still exists – and that is my truth.

Perhaps healing is not meant to be grand,

but in these small efforts, I still take a stand.

Evidence

I didn't know that I'd been healing —

not until I shut the door with care.

No cracking voice, no final pleading,

just peace that settled in the air.

The ache returned, as it still tries,

but this time, I did not invite

it in for tea beneath my eyes

or let it pull me into the night.

I reached for comfort, out of habit,

but found my own hand there instead —

not trembling like a startled rabbit,

just steady, warm, and gently fed.

The past remains — it doesn't sever —

but no longer asks for sacrifice.

And that, I think, is my first ever

proof that the cost was worth the price.

I no longer flinch at quiet mornings,

or brace myself for joy to end.

There's space between the subtle warnings,

and I no longer fear the bend.

I may still break — I often bend —

but softer now, and not alone.

There's peace in how I touch the end

of things, and still call this my own.

Where You Find Me

You didn't fix the broken ground,

but stayed beside where pain was found.

You knelt with me in tangled green,

and saw the beauty in the unseen.

You laughed like sunshine through the trees,

you quieted storms with playful ease.

Your love grew wild, not trimmed or tight —

a freckled spark, a soft delight.

You never asked me to be less,

just held my mess without distress.

With every joke and crooked grin,

you pulled the light back in again.

A soul I've known from lives before,

who wandered back to me once more.

And in each lifetime yet to be,

I'll plant my roots where you find me.

You never asked for something new,

just stayed and held what I'd been through.

You made the silence feel like grace,

and every scar a softer place.

You make me trust the threads of fate,

in doors unopened, paths we'll create.

You make me trust in quiet ways —

next time, always, and countless days.

Epilogue

And here, at the end, I find myself still standing – not because I have been healed, but because I have learned to carry the weight. There is strength in surviving, in facing what has been broken and still choosing to walk through it. This journey does not end with a perfect whole, but with the quiet recognition that there is beauty in imperfection. I hope these words find you as you are – scarred, strong, and full of possibility. For in our brokenness, we are never truly alone.

What Remains

Once, I was only fragments,

a name whispered in the wind,

a shadow caught between light and loss.

I have walked through ruins,

built monuments from grief,

planted gardens in the cracks of all I've lost.

And still, the wind sings my name.

Still, the light finds my skin.

Still, I remain.

Whole in a way I never expected,

broken in a way that no longer defines me.

The mosaic was never ruined.

It was waiting to be seen.

www.ingramcontent.com/pod-product-compliance
Lightning Source LLC
Chambersburg PA
CBHW031253120626
46545CB00007B/2789